SLEEK
FOR THE
LONG FLIGHT

RANDOM HOUSE
New York

new poems by
WILLIAM MATTHEWS

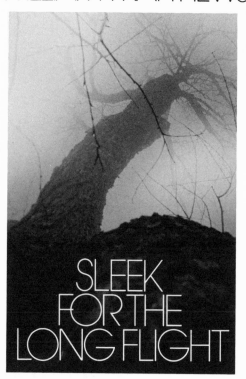

SLEEK
FOR THE
LONG FLIGHT

Acknowledgment is extended to the following publications in which these poems originally appeared:

Abraxas: For "Walking the Vineyards in August"
The Brown Bag: For "My Friends' Marriages Fly Apart Like Badly Designed Planes"
Carolina Quarterly: For "A Field Made Visible by Lightning"
Chelsea: For "Talk"
Choice: For "Letter to Russell Banks," "Two Wine-Making Poems"
Crazy Horse: For "Country Life," "Driving Alongside the Housatonic River Alone on a Rainy April Night."
December: For "Care"
Desert Review: For "And So" (originally entitled "And So You Grow")
The Dragonfly: For "The City of Silence"
Epoch: For "The Cat," "Sleeping Alone"
Field: For "Snow," "Stone"
Greensboro Review: For "Mother and Child"
Hearse: For "Attention, Everyone," "The Crossing," "Scorpio," "Underdog"
Kayak: For "Directions," "Marriage"
The Lamp in the Spine: For "Becoming a Woman"
The Nation: For "May Day"
New American Review: For "Ball and Chain, Yes Indeed," "Hard Stuff," "Night Driving," "Sleep," "Suppose"
Ohio Review: For "An Egg in the Corner of One Eye," "La Tache 1962"
Pebble: For "The Calculus," "Two New-Born Pigs"
Poetry: For "The Visionary Picnic"
Rapport #2: For "Praise," "Your Eyes, Your Name"
The Red Clay Reader: For "Narcissus Blues"
Roy Rogers: For "The Needle's Eye, The Lens"
St. Andrews Review: For "Another Beer"
The Stone: For "The Invention of Astronomy"
Sumac: For "A Prayer for the Pear Tree" (originally entitled "Climbing the Pear Tree"), "The Snake"
Tennessee Poetry Journal: For "Down to Sleep," "The Music Pool"
"The Moon" was first published in broadsheet form by Bruce Guernsey's Penyeach Press, Baltimore, Maryland.

ISBN 0-394-47969-6
Library of Congress Catalogue Card Number: 72-37065

Designed by Antonia Krass   Photo by Karen Becker
Manufactured in the United States of America
First Edition
9 7 5 3 2 4 6 8

Each thing's an end of something else:
I cannot hear a fainting pulse:
Farewell, loose metaphysic skin:
I would be out: you want me in . . .

Roethke

CONTENTS

FOUR

FIVE

SIX

SEVEN

ONE

Directions

The new road runs into
the old road, turn
west when your ankles hurt.
The wind will be thinning itself
in the grass. Listen, those thuds
are bees drunk with plunder
falling from the minarets of flowers
like ripe prayers.
Follow the path
their bodies make. Faster.
The dirt in that wineglass
came from Chateau d'Yquem.
You're getting closer.
That pile of clothes
is where some women
enter the river. Hurry up.
The last hill is called
Sleep's Kneecap, nobody
remembers why.
This is where the wind turns
back. From the ridge
you can see the light.
It's more like a bright soot,
really, or the dust
a moth's wing leaves
on the thumb and forefinger.
This is where I turn
back—you go the rest of the way
by eating the light until
there is none and the next one
eats along the glow
of your extinguished hunger and turns
to the living.

TWO

Scorpio

You are unpredictable, obsessed by sex and death, eager to assert your individuality. You can be devious, but charming. You will not be invited to the party. You carry your young on your back, because your tail cannot reach there and, instinctively, they know that. You wish they would get off.

If you were born today, you would have been a great basketball player except for the accident. Today's Scorpio daughter will be beautiful and intense: when her wishes are granted, she's in trouble.

When two of you are gathered in my name, your tails will snarl in the air like incestuous lariats. You should take care of that pressing financial obligation today. You have forgotten something. What do you think it is? You are a spine whose legs have failed to evolve into ribs.

Your conversation is only about you: you never mention me. I am the one who made you what you are. It is my fault. Tonight should be devoted to romantic pursuits. Whom shall we chase? We will not be invited to the party. You ought to forget about me. You tend to be careless of others. You are the only one I have ever loved.

Becoming a Woman

> *A man writing a poem is speaking to a woman inside him. That explains the common notion that a male poet is lecherous, homosexual or both. Why not say it this way: he wants to be whatever is other: a frog's tongue, an island formed by a volcano, the opposite sex, someone who loves him, the universe.*
>
> Jean-Phillipe Butron

All morning I watch how
my hands love each other
by releasing something else.
I'm the only one who can
forgive me for those I have loved.
I'm becoming a woman.

I lie all afternoon
in dry grass to hear
the insects whir
around me like fish
circling a wreck.
My time isn't my own.
Soon you'll be coming home.

What's wrong with me?
I can't explain. I feel like
a moon in a sack, a bass
bent against the current like a leer,
a dog with a cold rope.
Where have you been?
A bowl of thirst,
some words.
Listen, big boy, you know
those love poems of yours?
The only places I could live
in them are silences.

I leave a light on
in the bathroom for the moth.
You give me your body,
that ark
with one of every kind of animal.
I want to weep, as if
sleeping meant
entering an onion.
I grow thicker. I will be
my coach and my destination.

The City of Silence

As far as a sound wave rings out
before it's heard,
that's where the city limits are.

I keep the place clean.
Anything you worship
will let you be its priest.

If I open my mouth
a word falls in.
Gods avoid their shrines.

The streets are paved with streets.
Sleep is my radio and all
its news is true.

Sleeping Alone

A man is a necessity. A girl's mother says so by the way her hands come together after certain conversations, like a diary being closed.

But a boy's mother tells him *a woman is a luxury.* Maybe when he graduates his mother hugs him and forgets herself, she bites his earlobe! She remembers the hockey skates she gave him for Christmas when he was eight; the stiff flaps in back of the ankles resembled monks' cowls. The year before, the road froze over—they seemed to be what he should want.

Meanwhile the girl grows older, she hasn't been eight for ten years, her father is cruel to her mother. She'll always have a man, the way she likes to have in her room, even when visiting, a sandalwood box for her rings and coins, and a hand-painted mug showing two geese racing their reflections across a lake.

Maybe she will meet the boy, maybe not. The story does not depend on them. In a dark room a couple undress. She has always liked men's backs and holds on with her fingertips, like suction cups, turning one cheek up to him and staring through the dark across the rippled sheet. He breathes in her ear—some women like that. Or maybe they've loved each other for years and the lights are on. It doesn't matter; soon they will be sleeping.

Why do we say we *slept with* someone? The eyelids fall. It isn't *the one you love* or anyone else you recognize who says the only words you will remember from the dream. It must be the dream speaking, or the pope of all dreams speaking for the church. It says, *It's OK, we're only dying.*

Ball and Chain, Yes Indeed

It's all feeling.

Janis Joplin

Death's bread is still rising.
So much for food.
It's bad enough that
my breath is spliced
to the breath of the dead.
A barge of perfect garbage
arrives for re-cycling.
I hate this: I'm going to give
your gift away.
I hope I don't love
whomever's next.
I can feel the braid of my breath
fray. I'll ruin my voice
with this warning.
Cut me loose, I love you
too much.

Hard Stuff

You know the way they say "on drugs,"
the dilettantes?
You learn one
well, that prickle
the lines in your palms make
retracting, pulling
the little fat that's left
over them for the night.
There's no plural. The hands
hate one another.

The Calculus

There is a culture which counts like this: "one, two, many." It is sufficient. They don't use numbers to measure. There are so many women your wife gets pushed out of bed. Everyone knows without a name for it how many dead men a camel can carry. There is so little light the dark part of each eye grows knuckle-size.

The invention of zero will end their life. They don't say "no moon tonight"; they say "the moon is gone." We can add this egg of absence to anything —then we are richer.

The Moon

They call it snow
but I know it's your light,
wafer of burnt earth.
An owl in the larch shuffles
his feathers once and sleeps.

It's the old indifference, the calm
of loving nothing.
Let the amino acids
have the universe.

Driving Alongside the Housatonic River Alone on a Rainy April Night

I remember asking
where does my shadow go at night?
I thought it went home,
it grew so sleek at dusk.
They said, you just don't
notice it, the way you don't tell yourself
how to walk or hear
a noise that doesn't stop.
But one wrong wobble
in the socket and inside the knee
chalk is falling, school
is over.
As if the ground were a rung
suddenly gone from a ladder,
the self, the shoulders bunched
against the road's each bump, the penis
with its stupid grin,
the whole rank slum of cells
collapses.
I feel the steering wheel
tug a little, testing.
For as long as that takes
the car is a sack of kittens
weighed down by stones.
The headlights chase a dark ripple
across some birch trunks.
I know it's there, water
hurrying over the shadow of water.

Another Beer

The first one was for the clock
and its one song
which is the song's name.

Then a beer for the scars in the table,
all healed in the shape of initials.

Then a beer for the thirst
and its one song we keep forgetting.

And a beer for the hands
we are keeping to ourselves.
The body's dogs, they lie
by the ashtray and thump
suddenly in their sleep.

And a beer for our reticence,
the true tongue, the one song,
the fire made of air.

Then a beer for the juke box.
I wish it had the recording
of a Marcel Marceau mime performance:
28 minutes of silence,
2 of applause.

And a beer for the phone booth.
In this confessional you can sit.
You sing it your one song.

And let's have a beer for whoever goes home
and sprawls, like the remaining sock,
in the drawer of his bed and repeats
the funny joke and pulls it
shut and sleeps.

And a beer for anyone
who can't tell the difference between
death and a good cry
with its one song.
None of us will rest enough.

The last beer is always for the road.
The road is what the car drinks
travelling on its tongue of light
all the way home.

THREE

Night Driving

You follow into their dark tips
those two skewed tunnels of light.
Ahead of you, they seem to meet.
When you blink, it is the future.

Two Wine-Making Poems

for Robert Morgan

1. Fining with Egg Whites

So much like the light-traceries
inside a closed eyelid,
egg whites sink in their thickening nets
unconverted yeasts
and other particles.
The wine is cleared, dark.
Something swimming on this pond
took its web of ripples
to the bottom.

2. Fermenting Vat

It takes two to clean it.
One stays outside because
one alone grows stunned and finally
drunk inside
this cylinder of petrified wine—
oak so dense with essence
of Pinot Noir the stain is now the wood.
The lung remembers its life as a tree.
You can't imagine blood this black.

The Needle's Eye, the Lens

Here comes the blind thread to sew it shut.

Suppose

The future isn't out there
waiting,
nor is the past snail-slime
(like Heisenberg's particle
it is deflected
by the light we see it by).

And sperm survive so long
an unfaithful woman
sometimes carries home
dead letters still alive,
foxfire, broken code.

Or, "Time
like a pacing coach
frets the field away."
Suppose the universe
is running down, a clockful
of dying crickets.
Downward to darkness on extended
metaphor.
In the History of Ideas
everything Good is Done For.

Yet
light like a stream
of liquid beads
drills into open eyes
across a space its flowing
strings.
        To blink implies
muscular faith:

there isn't time for much
to change
                 and
blood loops like a tape
recording of great prayers
about the blood,
about the blood.

An Egg in the Corner of One Eye

I can only guess what it contains. I lean to the mirror like a teen-ager checking his complexion. Maybe it is sleep. Or a dream in which, like a bee or nursing mother or a radish, you eat to feed others. Or maybe it is a shard of light in the shape of an island from which dogs are leaping into the water, swimming toward a barking that only death can hear. On the eye's other shore life is upside-down. The dogs have swum for days to clamber up and, like an eye in its deathbed, shake out rays of light. Or maybe the light implodes. Or sinks into itself like a turned-off TV, the optic nerve subsiding like a snapped kitestring. I don't know. To open a tear is to kill whatever it was growing. I can't tell the difference between grief and joy. I tell myself that a tear is my death, leaking. In this way weeping resembles menstruation. The egg that will be fertilized never sees the light of day.

Narcissus Blues

Charity, come home,
begin.

W. S. Merwin

When you rest your hands
on the table they rattle
like dice full of gamblers.
It's too long between feedings.
Then your wife is there, too,
begging for love, and while you explain
the soup gets dirty.
It's that damn gas heat
and she begins to snuffle
and calls you a toad
in a loud voice with the windows open.

It's as if you too could be
poor or insane
or need somebody
to hit, and your precise agonies
are nothing, and the brotherhood of pain
is spurious, and your tongue curls
like a harem slipper.
You're going to shave a stranger
backwards every morning
and not a word of thanks.

You loathe your sensible underwear,
your old songs & old girlfriends.
It's time you had a life
of your own.
May you wake in your body
like a drunk alone in a lifeboat,
a sealed letter
from your dead mother.

My Friends' Marriages Fly Apart
Like Badly Designed Planes

The hills gleam shards.
A bee's eye broken by refraction.
Maybe lies keep the marriage up

until they grow a sheath
of ice. The Air Force paid
for a study which showed the bumblebee

can't fly,
aerodynamically speaking.
Suppose he is scared to death

and going home?
I've watched the blades
of your shoulders cut

toward each other
like a suicidal bat's.
I tell you,

it made my landing gear
retract.
And I can't forget

the delicious shimmy in *my* wings,
the thickening echo of my
engine bouncing back up faster.

There's no way we can crash
except together.
We're my favorite biplane.

One hand on the stick,
Big Boy, you remind me.
We push through the wet night

air, through the space we take up
flying, carrying like a sack of mail
our undelivered futures.

Mother and Child

What's this? he is
uncapping his camera.
He wants you

so posed that above your thatch
of pale short hair the light
blurs beautifully.

You are embarrassed.
The lens is open a long time.
You will be what he wants

to see. You despair.
O when the sun goes down
like a doomed and lyrical ship,

a little loaf of light will rise
in the sea's dark pan.
There you are,

he says. He calls it you.
As long as he loves it
you are free. You call it you.

You need a father for it,
should you ask him to marry you?
Staring into its eyes,

your own are full.
It is the moon of your new night.

May Day

Finches flower on the lilac
noisily, the dogwood blossoms turn
in a night from a dull, muddy ivory
to white skin of the princess.
She must marry her father's friend,
the one with the hairy back.
In the streets: catarrh
of tanks or husbands,
force pridefully restrained.
And under the girl's thin dress
the vine of her body is growing on her.
They will live long together,
they will never marry.
The hair will fall from men like rust
and she and the sure body
will lie down together. Listen,
she is singing to it.

Marriage

Sleeping late, I float in bed.
What you can see may be
the top of seventy feet of kelp
sewn to the murky floor.
Whatever has pushed me all these
years from that slime,
I'm still its slow explosion.
You bob beside me. Time to do
death's work gratefully.
Wake up. We are one
of each other's tasks.
We drift on our tethers.
Death's work is boring
but dangerous. To pass the time
we fall in love and out
and in. . . . Our cells get used
to this music.

The Invention of Astronomy

The eyelids fall, the star-charts.

Down to Sleep

When it thundered Papa
turned a mild eye to the sky
and counted: *one thousand
and one, one thousand
and two. . . .* The dog whimpered.
Blue light skewed down the sky,
corkscrews of energy and burnt
air, nosefuls of ozone.
Half an oak peeled back
like lilac bark. The current
slurred in the walls and the radio
lowered its voice. *Bedtime,*
I thought it said, and down the shaft
of sleep I lowered my crackling
body, past the jagged seams.
Silt replaced my marrow.
The last light I knew
grew in ferns of blood inside
my eyelids.
Into the slime my dark flame
spiralled and I was
spent, absent,
mine.

FOUR

Praise

First, to the feet, as they bear what you have grown
    to live in, your pod of a body, slow to explode.

And to the toes, as they were roots once, and so you
    go by me like a bush of bells searching for
    music, and I sing in my bad voice *hello* and
    we turn to each other.

And to the calves, as their long canoe-shaped mus-
    cles glide in the same place always over the
    sunken bone, the body's future.

And to the knees, as they are loud echoes of the
    knuckles and the backs of them grow pink and
    painful if you fall asleep face-down in the sun.

When the thighs are drunk on duty and I creep by, I
    tell them a strange dream and they have it and
    are refreshed. Praise to the thighs, stolid and
    lovely.

And to the buttocks, as they bob like pans of a scale
    when you walk away and take my true weight
    when I lie down on you.

And to the hips, as every cup should have a handle,
    as they are the ears and ankles of the body's
    delta, as they are your calcium outriggers cov-
    ered by flesh.

And to the navel, as it is the first crater. Its seal is
    all that's left of your mother's letter explaining
    happiness and pain. Praise to the navel.

And to the *linea alba,* as it is bellrope for the pubic
    hair and the tongue's path to music lessons.

And to the clitoris, as it is a loaf of tiny bread, a
   pearl of blood, because it does nothing but
   drum and trouble the inner waters.

And to the cunt, as it is the glove that is mother to
   the finger, mouth that gives speech to the
   tongue, home that gives restlessness to the
   cock.

And to the stomach, as it contains the speech your
   body makes to itself, boring as can be, every
   day of hunger: *Fill me, I am empty with the
   knowledge of my need.*

And to the back, as the dunes of muscles shift
   across it, and that underground river of bones,
   your spine, flows through it.

And to the shoulders, as they were wings once.
   Your shoulders gather like dense clouds that
   are moored by rain to the rest of your body,
   and I praise the way they float there.

And to the breasts, as they doze waiting for babies,
   as the nipples sting in cold wind, as a hand or
   tongue, like a shadow with the right weight,
   passes over them.

And to the throat, as it is the stalk of your face and
   the place where your breath breaks into the
   right syllables: I place my tongue on your
   throat's bluest vein, in praise.

And to the tongue, as it lolls and darts on its tether
   —domestic, secret, blunt.

And to the lips, as my name or anything you say blooms on them to die away. When I kiss you I leave my name again for your breath to pass through.

And to the nose, as it remembers and uses fumes from the fire of the arriving future.

And to the ears, as their delicate bones shiver precisely; they are shells listening to themselves, and they can hear the roar of the blood always.

When I stare into your eyes, a little knot of light in mine breaks. Undressing the light, we see that darkness is its birthmark. Praise to the eyes.

And to the hair, as when I sift it with my fingers it remembers its first life as grass on the early earth and springs back to its own shape.

And to the arms, as they hold in order to let go. We rock in the boats of our bodies. The wind rises, the final lust. When you raise your arms, the space between them is a sail I helped to sew.

And to the hands, as their cargo of scars and air can never be given away. You may rest them on my body if you like.

And to the fingers, as they are failed tunnels into nothingness. They went a little way and came home to the body.

And to the bones, the body's ore and its memory of itself when the rest of it is the breath of something else—to the bones, praise.

And to the face, as light flares and calms between
the skin and skull. And those blind cows, my
fingers, graze there in any weather.

And to the blood, tireless needle pulling its thread of
tides, tireless praise. Say it again and again,
the names are lying down to sleep together.

The Cat

While you read
the sleepmoth begins
to circle your eyes
and then—
a hail of claws
lands the cat
in your lap.
The little motor
in his throat
is how a cat says
Me. He rasps the soft
file of his tongue
along the inside
of your wrist.
He licks himself.
He's building
a pebble of fur
in his stomach.
And now he pulls
his body in a circle
around the fire of sleep.

This is the wet
sweater with legs
that shakes in
from the rain,
split-ear the sex burglar,
Fish-breath, Wind-
minion, paw-poker
of dust
tumbleweeds,
the cat that kisses
with the wet
flame of his tongue
each of your eyelids
as if sealing
a letter.

One afternoon
napping under the light-
ladder
let down by the window,
there are two of them:
cat and cat-
shadow, sleep.

One night you lay your book
down like the clothes
your mother wanted
you to wear tomorrow.
You yawn.
The cat exhales a moon.
Opening a moon,
you dream of cats.
One of them strokes you
the wrong way. Still,
you sleep well.

This is the same cat
Plunder.
This is the old cat
Milk-whiskers.
This is the cat
eating one of its lives.
This is the first cat
Fire-fur.
This is the next cat
St. Sorrow.
This is the cat with its claws
furled, like sleep's flag.
This is the lust cat
trying to sleep with its shadow
This is the only cat
I have ever loved.
This cat has written
in tongue-ink
the poem you are reading now,
the poem scratching
at the gate of silence,
the poem
that forgives
itself
for its used-up lives,
the poem
of the cat waking,
running a long shudder
through his body,
stretching again,
following the moist bell
of his nose
into the world
again.

FIVE

Talk

The body is never silent. Aristotle said that we can't hear the music of the spheres because it is the first thing that we hear, blood at the ear. Also the body is brewing its fluids. It is braiding the rope of food that moors us to the dead. Because it sniffles and farts, we love the unpredictable. Because breath goes in and out, there are two of each of us and they distrust each other. The body's reassuring slurps and creaks are like a dial tone: we can always call up the universe. And so we are always talking. My body and I sit up late, telling each other our troubles. And when two bodies are near each other, they begin talking in body-sonar. The art of conversation is not dead! Still, for long periods, it is comatose. For example, suppose my body doesn't get near enough to yours for a long time. It is disconsolate. Normally it talks to me all night: listening is how I sleep. Now it is truculent. It wants to speak directly to your body. The next voice you hear will be my body's. It sounds the same way blood sounds at your ear. It is saying *Ssshhh,* now that we, at last, are silent.

Care

You are almost happy.
Your eyes swerve like two birds
spurting from a car's path.
Looking into your face
is like seeing light
through a leaf. Is there any way
to hold you without pinning
those wings, the shadows
of your shoulder blades?

A Prayer for the Pear Tree

Climbing the pear tree
to save it from wild grape,
we find precious little heartwood left
alive,
the lulled sap thickening
inside the clasped branches.

Grape leaves shred light.

Like clumps of sweat
the grape berries shrivel
back into themselves.

It is like ripping flesh away,
the pear and grape
have lived so long together.

At night the pear tree rattles
remembering its glove of grape.

A tense clench, fist
of foxfire still growing from the wrist.

May the snake of sleep straighten,
may the bare
pear branches knit recklessly like bones in milk,
in moonlight,
in new pale air
we've cleared around them,
you and I.

Your Eyes, Your Name

1.

These words we have swallowed—
blind fish in an underground lake.
One dies up into your eyes
like a stone bubble.
Love offers miraculous
exactions. I lean to this dank
flame of no fire,
I try to name it.

2.

More light, I cried, as Goethe
did from his deathbed.
It sounded beautiful and true.
But it's one thing to go blind
if you're about to die.
And here I am, two frank
explosions in your eyes.
This close you become—in its
fervency—the light I give you back.
Now I know what to say:
your name, true title
to this poem. I'll love you
as well as you'll let me.
More light. More darkness, too.

3.

So it must be late
afternoon, kiss me.
Your small mouth is beautiful.
Your eyes close.
Tongues, eels
of shy light—they are names
learning to pronounce each other.

4.

Now it's night. Our light
is prickling through it
like fire along the veins
of a deserted coal mine.
A storm would be appropriate.
After a storm the earth
and I are delirious with ease.
I close my eyes.

Lightning chars the air sweet
and original, and so does sleep.

5.

I'd like to name a book of poems
Foreplay. One poem unbuttons
your interpretation of it.
Another's breath smells of a toothpaste blended
from raspberries and Romanée-Conti, 1959,
and this poem is the best kisser.
Another is a hand of light
staining a dark breast.
One is a willful tongue
and will creep anywhere along your body.
Each poem has a beautiful hobby.
They are like blankets we have kicked away,
a mound
knit from the last notes
sung before the silence
these poems have always loved.

And So

        you grow
in your cocoon of sleep,
like a dead sailor
revived inside his flag.

The Visionary Picnic

These memories of what
is about to happen, silences
the old dog Frostbite has just left. . . .
The tiny valleys of his pawprints—

so much like the black
empty lakes on dice—
fill with snow or moonlight
or some white thing or bone.

Remember the night the moon-
crescent was on its back
like a melon-rind or runner
of a rocking chair? The snow

seemed to be falling up,
smoke from silence's fire.
You watched as if your life
were being told in code.

Suppose you have an angel,
a shadow made of light
and reticence? Woman
be consoled by your strangeness, by

its ceremonies.
There's snow on the sandwiches.
Only a song you have never imagined
or the oil of the right harsh herb

can melt this meal of guilt
and stuttering intentions.
You begin a speech on
"pleasant pressures." It was

supposed to come out "present pleasures"
but never mind, already the snow is
in ascent and we're becoming food,
each body dark with hunger

to be eaten. We lie
down in the sandwiches.
The world is strange.
Look in our eyes and see.

The Music Pool

You have to put your head in.
It's so much like silence
it takes all your breath
to begin
hearing it. Then you never forget
the sound of being held
completely still by someone you love.
Soon you will undress
but not yet.

Attention, Everyone

Gloom is the enemy, even to the end. The parodies of self-knowledge were embossed by Gloom inside our eyelids, and the abrasion makes us weep, for no reason, like a new bride disconsolate in the nightgown she had sewn so carefully. The dog comes back from the fields, lumpy with burrs. I put down my pen and pull them out; it is a care I have taught him to expect. I've always said it would be difficult.

I'm declaring a new regime. Its flag is woven loam. Its motto is: *Love is worth even its own disasters*. Its totem is the worm. We eat our way through grief and make it richer. We don't blunt ourselves against stones—their borders go all the way through. We go around them. In my new regime Gloom dances by itself, like a sad poet.

Also I will be sending out some letters: Dear Friends, Please come to the party for my new life. The dog will meet you at the road, barking, running stiff-legged circles. Pluck one of his burrs and follow him here. I've got lots of good wine, I'm in love, my new poems are better than my old poems. It's been too long since we started over.

The new regime will start when you lift your eyes from this page. Here it comes.

SIX

Walking the Vineyards in August

The grape-clumps sag,
dowsing. Roots wet,
roots laborious:
I'm only passing through.
My bones stunt in their tunnels
and grow crisp. I carry
them everywhere.
They want out.

I come here every year
looking for death's equivalent
to the genetic code.
Wine from these grapes
fat with their own sugars—
I will be drinking it.
I'll buy a case.

Pulling each cork
will be like breaking open half
a pair of dice—its final
number will fall out.
I should have known.

The Snake

A snake is the love of a thumb
and forefinger.
Other times, an arm
that has swallowed a bicep.

The air behind this one
is like a knot
in a child's shoelace
come undone
while you were blinking.

It is bearing something away.
What? What time
does the next snake leave?

This one's tail is ravelling
into its burrow—
a rosary returned to a purse.
The snake is the last time your spine
could go anywhere alone.

Underdog

A 95-lb. German Shepherd
trained against violence:
that cringe, that fish
on four stilts
has survived evolution.

My thumb had to be broken
before it would bend.
He wags his whole body.
I look in his eyes
and understand nothing.
Where is my reflection?
Dogs see in grey.

When he runs on the road
failed bone blunts into his paws.
That dog
sleeps at the foot of the bed.

Woodchuck-breath, plow-snout,
boundary walker,
the muscles get used to their use.
Stiff-legs, we grow dead
outward, like a tree.

The Crossing

Seen from below,
two knees praying themselves pale
are a pair of bald men seasick
over the same rail.
This wake, this lisp of foam
is always here, dog
made of moonspume on the water.

As a cake of Ivory soap
skims over the raised ridges
of an old-timey washboard,
so does this ship skip
o'er the wave-tips,
fare thee well.
Port outward, starboard home.

How can a strawberry for breakfast
three days out be "fresh"?
What's happening to my mind?
Only the imagination is real.
Why does each of these stanzas
have seven lines?
The water is always leaping aside

as would a grasshopper
from the shadow of a falling foot.
Or a craven dog: O
Moonslaver, Waterclaws, Bow-Wow—
I don't love you anymore.
Who's feeding whom?
Water, what do you want of me now?

La Tache 1962

for Michael Cuddihy

Pulling the long cork, I shiver with a greed so pure it is curiosity. I feel like the long muscles in a sprinter's thighs when he's in the blocks, like a Monarch butterfly the second before it begins migrating to Venezuela for the winter—I feel as if I were about to seduce somebody famous. Pop. The first fumes swirl up. In a good year the Domaine de la Romanée-Conti gets maybe 20,000 bottles of La Tache; this is number 4189 for 1962. In the glass the color is intense as if from use or love, like a bookbinding burnished by palm-oil. The bouquet billows the sail of the nose: it is a wind of loam and violets. "La tache" means "the task." The word has implications of piecework; perhaps the vineyard workers were once paid by the chore rather than by the day. In a good year there would be no hail in September. Work every day. Finally, the first pressing of sleep. Stems, skins, a few spiders, yeast-bloom and dust-bloom on the skins. . . . Now the only work is waiting. On the tongue, under the tongue, with a slow breath drawn over it like a cloud's shadow—, the wine holds and lives by whatever it has learned from 3½ acres of earth. What I taste isn't the wine itself, but its secrets. I taste the secret of thirst, the longing of matter to be energy, the sloth of energy to lie down in the trenches of sleep, in the canals and fibres of the grape. The day breaks into cells living out their secrets. Marie agrees with me: this empty bottle number 4189 of La Tache 1962 held the best wine we have ever drunk. It is the emblem of what we never really taste or know, the silence all poems are unfaithful to. Michael, suppose the task is to look on until our lives have given themselves away? Amigo, Marie and I send you our love and this poem.

Two New-born Pigs

One is dull black, the other the same slick orange-pink a cheap rubber football gets when wet. After the sheep are done—now that the fairs are over they are all the color of plowed city snow browned by car exhaust—the pigs eat what is left. Each day, like tiny planes battering dirty clouds, they circle the sheeps' rumps. If one tries to slither underneath, a sheep sits on him and goes on weaving grain into its body. The trough they finally reach used to be barn-siding. They sweep their small snouts over what remains.

Country Life

for Michael Benedikt

Sowing a row of Early Wonder
Beets, let's say, or a border
of nasturtiums, you stop
to wonder where you're travelling
by knee.
Into the August tool-shed musk,
into a fermenting apple.

There goes the plow sealing
with a new two-foot snowbank
the driveway you cleared all morning.
There go the geese back to the lake
after their dusk feeding
on corn-stubble:
it must be March:
next they go north to nest.
And if you lie flat and silent
you can hear the suburbs coming
on their elbows.

The stones dance in place.
On one of them a mole is knocking
but it won't come out, this
is its day for dancing.

A Field Made Visible by Lightning

If energy is our god,
we have learned again to fear him.
This one short poem he has sent us—
so much like those texts burnt
into our palms—is too much.
We had been praying for it.

It is one of those moments
when the brain seems to swell,
to shudder
like a chick in an egg—stunned
by what it cannot understand.
Two ravens rise from an open book
making evolution simple.
The brain wants out.

Stone

for Charles Simic

The creek has made its bed
and wants to lie in it.
That's why spring is terrifying.
Water rises like the bloated drowned
against the ice. In the churn
stones are born stunned.

And at night:
the house, rising
like a cliff of fire.
There were the trees, mobiles
of shale, and the grass
like a field of tiny gravestones growing wild.
And the moon, a stone fruit
hoping to be opened,
its 28 sections of stolen light
flying home.

In the streambed, a stone
shaped by watersurge:
it looks like the ankle bone
of a lost species grown too graceful.
Evolution makes us sleek
for the long flight.
Finally our common life breaks open,
a pod releasing its stone peas,
and the earth bears in a few places
a few wrinkles in our shapes
for a few million years.

Snow

The dog's spine, like a dolphin's,
sews a path
through the smaller drifts.
These graying roadside lumps,
like sheets waiting to be washed. . . .
You have to press 4,000 snowgrapes
for one bottle of this winter light.
A white moss girdles
every tree.
          All the erased
roads lead north, into the wind.
The house is a sack of sour breath
on the earth's back.
Glass drumskins
in the windows quiver.

I stare in a stupor of will,
fleck-faced, bearing my cow of a body
easily on the earth.
Intricate adjustments in my inner ears
and the gravitational habits of planets
keep me steady.
It's nothing personal, I know,
but so much basic work is being done for me
I ought to stop whining.

Sky shreds,
woods fade
like an old grainy photograph.
Slick white gearwheels mesh
and turn:
                which is what makes the hiss.
It is the suck and sigh
of shattered air
hoping to be ocean.
It is the glut of snow that I love.
A snowpelt
grows on the mailbox, the Volvo, the dog.
When I turn up
my eyes, my snow
rises to meet the snow.

Sleep

Last cough,
lungcells six hours safe from cigarettes.
The testicles drone
in their hammocks,
making sperm.
Glut and waste
and then the beach invasion,
people
everywhere, the earth in its regular
whirl slurring to silence
like a record at the onset
of a power failure.
I'm burning ferns to heat my house.
I am
The Population Bomb, no,
not a thing but a process:
fire: fire.

Ashes and seeds.
Now in my drowse I want to spend,
spend before the end.
Sleep with a snowflake,
wake with a wet wife.
This is the dream in which the word "pride"
appears as a comet.
Its tail is the whole language
you tried as a child to learn.

Difficult and flashy dreams!
But they're all
allegory, like that comet.
You can turn your head fast
and make the light smear,
and you wake to watch it
staining the windows, good
stunned morning, people
everywhere, all of us
unravelling, it's so good
to be alive.

SEVEN

Letter to Russell Banks

Ithaca
January Thaw 1971

Dear Russ,
            Another daughter! Old friend
you are indeed pillowed
by love of women. As I walk
all the woodlands for sale
near Ithaca, trolling for the land
that will lure me
down like a dowser's wand,
I feel the fist in all of us
opening. On the palm—
a tiny fist like a pink lettuce-head.
Our children are the only message
we can leave them.

Solstice, pivot of faded light.
But now it's ooze and spreading edges,
40° and down to 10° at night,
cars slurring lanes on the slick
morning roads, the day-long
drip from the eaves. The stiff
shrivelled berries of the yew
burn free from the snow.
My greed for land swells
like a tic. Creek water leaks
to the surface.

Spiked by a slim maple:
a huge hornet's nest,
serene, a blank face
waiting to be minted.
Thinking of a new house means
re-defining love.
Nobody knows how deep
we'll have to drill the well.

Stepping into woods, I think
of my ancestors and how Wales
and Norway are slivers in the globe.
I dwindle into the woods
and know why they were terrified.
Nobody knew Jamestown
stretched to the Pacific Ocean.
So you cut down a tree,
made a stake, beat it
into the earth and
hung on as a flag.
The wilderness was
too large then for us to love,
as is the city now.
Wilderness, here we come
again, ants dragging
a bulldozer, a sewer
like a gut straightened out.
Deep in the woods now
I spin suddenly to surprise
and see whatever follows me.
It is the memory of a tail,
the thrash of its absence.

Fish-in-the-wrist,
cloud-in-the-mouth,
go home.

I explain I'm looking for a home.

Stone-in-the-throat,
fern-foot,
fire burns wherever it goes.

All those dough-flecked hands
cupping one flame of solitude!
Mothers, girlfriends, wives
and daughters.
The spine like a lodgepole of fire.

                  yrs, burning outward,
                  Bill

About the Author

BILL MATTHEWS lives with his wife and two sons in the country outside Ithaca, New York. There he teaches writing courses at Cornell, edits the Lillabulero Press Poetry Pamphlet Series, and writes. His first book of poetry, *Ruining the New Road,* was published by Random House in 1970. Recently he has been working, with Mary Feeney, on translations from the prose poems of the late French poet Jean Follain. He has given readings of his poetry at numerous schools and colleges.